T0194940

RE-MAKE AN ICON

So You Can Produce One In Yourself & Others

Unique Use of Biography For Greater Achievement

Nanthalia McJamerson, Ph. D.

authorHOUSE®

AuthorHouse™
1663 Liberty Drive
Bloomington, IN 47403
www.authorhouse.com
Phone: 1 (800) 839-8640

Cover Design by Brandon Richardson

Published by AuthorHouse 05/23/2020

ISBN: 978-1-7283-1651-2 (sc)
ISBN: 978-1-7283-1650-5 (e)

Library of Congress Control Number: 2019908125

Print information available on the last page.

This book is printed on acid-free paper.

CONTENTS

TIMELINE FOR
THE PROJECT

Week 1

Preview before you begin the process: Read through the entire book to get a clear understanding of what this Project involves and requires. You will learn about the benefits, the goals and each step of the process in order to help you focus when you begin to read the autobiography. Then choose your Icon and find the autobiography or biography you want to study for this Project.

Week 2

Pay close attention to the definitions given in the **Matrix for Achieving Success Despite Extraordinary Challenges (MASDEC)**. The Matrix is the key to the entire Project. Because the definitions in the Matrix are central, they will be re-stated when you start on the worksheets in each category.

Week 3

Begin to follow the Directions page. Initially focus on Step 1 (READ) and Step 2 (ANALYZE) as you read about important events in your Icon's life. The **Problem Inventory** sheets and **Success Worksheets** will provide space for you to record your results. A brief example is provided of the information expected on each type of worksheet. Although the worksheets are listed in sequence, you do not have to follow that sequence because the Icon's life events may not unfold in a particular order. Continue to work on PART I of this book until you have completed your Icon's life story. Review the definitions and examples as needed: Ability Nutrition, Ambition Ignition, Cardiac Reserve, Apex Nerve, Insight Trams, and Opportunity Rams.

Week 4

Begin to work on Step 3: SPECULATE. Focus on completing the **Reconstruction Worksheets** on which you will re-write your Icon's life by following the instructions on the worksheet.

Week 5

This is the FUN part! Begin to work on Step 4: CREATE & SHARE. Use what you learned about your Icon from completing Steps 2 and 3 to create or produce something <u>original</u> and plan a way to share your creations according to the instructions in Step 4. Sharing will allow all participants to learn about several achievers and to be inspired.

Week 6

Either at the completion of your Icon's biography or at any point during your reading, you may begin work on PART II of this book: ALL ABOUT YOUR SUCCESS. Answer the questions in the same categories as you did in the study of your Icon. This section pushes you to grow.

Week 7

Begin to work on Step 5 (REFLECT). Use Exit Tickets 1 and 2 to reflect upon the Project experience. Finally, in Step 6 (ACTION), complete PART III: USING YOUR LESSONS TO HELP OTHERS. This section of the project will allow you to advance from a "Success Seeker to a Success Builder."

THE GOALS

At the end of this project, you will
1. See yourself and others as
VALUED
more
&
CAPABLE
of more
2. Know how to seek
and build capacity for
GREATER ACHIEVEMENT!

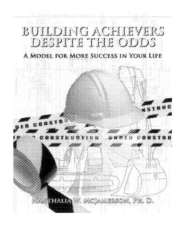

Dear Future Icon,

Yes, there is greatness within you! Biographies of your Icons hold important secrets about ways to realize your greatness. Biographies and autobiographies give you a day-by-day, blow-by-blow look at the struggles that someone had to overcome in order to become your Icon. In this *Re-Make an Icon* project, you will receive more than information about success secrets. You will increase your skills, have some fun, use your creativity and be empowered by lessons for your own future success.

Part I of this project guides you through a special process of looking for your Icon's problems then finding what it took to overcome those problems. The process is called "The Matrix for Achieving Success despite the Challenges." The process is based on six (6) types of "building materials" for greater achievement. Part II of this project will show you how to use those six materials in your life to make you more successful. In Part III, you will use what you will have learned in order to help others succeed.

Are you ready? Let's get started.

Respectfully,
Nanthalia McJamerson
(The General Contractor for Building Achievers)

RE-MAKE AN ICON SO YOU CAN PRODUCE ONE

"When I was a child, I had 21 mothers, and I needed every one of them. Each time I fell through a different crack, a different mother would catch me."

John Hurst Adams

This *Re-Make an Icon* Project will give you a new way to look at yourself as a "Future Icon" while you study your Icon's autobiography. You will re-make your Icon by investigating the details of his or her problems and discovering the solutions. The fun part will be re-writing his or her life story. For example, you can create "The Other Albert Einstein" or "The Other Oprah" or "The Other Beyonce". Later, you will investigate your life and learn to bring forth more of your own and others' potential greatness.

The Re-Make an Icon Project is based on the foundations of Human Development, Critical Pedagogy and Aesthetic Education. For more than 20 years, this project has helped hundreds of people (from teenagers to retirees) learn success secrets and tools while having fun working on higher achievement. If you complete the entire process, then you will see yourself and others as **Valued** and **Capable** of greater achievement.

Begin the Project by closely studying the "Matrix for Achieving Success Despite Extraordinary Challenges" (MASDEC). It explains the six success-building categories.

NOTE: For more details about the story of the project as well as the theories, research and impact of it, see the book titled *Reconstructing Lives: Taking the Mystery out of Success.*

"MATRIX FOR ACHIEVING SUCCESS"

Despite Extraordinary Challenges" (MASDEC)

Premise: Extraordinary structures are made of specific materials (titanium, polycarbonate glass, malleable metals). Extraordinary people are made of massive amounts of the following materials:

ABILITY NUTRITION: The requirement for someone or something to identify, reveal, protect and/or help develop specific talents, skills or capabilities of a person. Possession of ability is deficient if it is not recognized and nourished.

AMBITION IGNITION: The requirement for someone or something to initiate, generate and sustain motivation, inspiration, dreams or goals in a person's life. Behind determination is an attitude of "I will" that was preceded by the attitude of "I want".

CARDIAC RESERVE: The requirement for someone or something to cause a person to feel valued, loved or important. The emotional heart must be maintained with enough reserves of warmth and worth to prevent or heal emotional damage.

APEX NERVE: The requirement for someone or something to demand performance at a level of excellence in any given area. It requires someone or something to "push" a person. Excellence training is the development of proficiency or virtuosity rather than mere functionality. It is essential for maximizing potential.

INSIGHT TRAMS: The requirement for someone or something to move a person forward or closer to their dreams and goals by teaching them how to grow deeper in academic, emotional, financial or spiritual understanding. Progress toward success is proportionate to the amount of insight gained.

OPPORTUNITY RAMS: The requirement for someone or something to provide awareness of or resources for opportunities to assist with destroying obstacles to a person's progress. The existence of opportunity is useless for those who have neither awareness of nor access to those opportunities.

DIRECTIONS FOR "RE-MAKING" YOUR ICON

Your Icon's Name:_____

Your Name:_____

Step 1: <u>READ.</u> As you read the autobiography of the Icon (of your choice), complete the Project worksheets provided in this book.

Step 2: <u>ANALYZE.</u> Use the *Problem Inventory* sheets to list the MAJOR problems or challenges that this Icon faced related to each category. On the *Success Worksheet,* list and explain the MAJOR people, experiences and/or things which helped overcome the problems you identified. Provide evidence with page numbers.

Step 3: <u>SPECULATE.</u> Use the *Reconstruction Worksheets* to select one of the persons, experiences or things which you already identified in <u>Step 2</u>, and imagine what could have happened if that particular factor <u>had not been</u> a part of the Icon's life. Complete all three of the "Scripts for the Icon's New Life".

Step 4: <u>CREATE.</u> Based upon your work from Steps 2 and 3, create something original, such as a skit, rap, poem, hashtag, power-point, music, or visual art about your Icon. Share your creation in a small group or in a Talent Show.

Step 5: <u>REFLECT.</u> Use Exit Ticket #1 to explain how your study and Re-making of this Icon's life story helped you understand what is necessary for great achievement in spite of life challenges.

Step 6: <u>TAKE ACTION.</u> Use the Worksheets and Exit Ticket #2 in PART II to examine your life and work on your future success. Finalize the Project with PART III to empower others to succeed.

PART I

ALL ABOUT THE
SUCCESS OF YOUR ICON

"People will forget
What you said,
People will forget
What you did,
But people will
Never forget
How You made them feel."

Maya Angelou

1

ABILITY NUTRITION

ABILITY NUTRITION: The requirement for someone or something to identify, reveal, protect and/or help develop specific talents, skills or capabilities of a person. Possession of ability is deficient if it is not recognized and nourished.

Example of an Icon with Many Problems: In second grade, Michelle Obama had an incompetent teacher who did not like children. Michelle, therefore, was devalued and not learning.

Example of One Solution: Michelle's mother quietly campaigned for weeks to have her daughter tested and moved out of that classroom to one with a "smiling, no-nonsense teacher who knew her stuff." That "life-changing move" led to future school success.

PROBLEM INVENTORY #1

List and briefly explain at least two (2) of the MAJOR or SIGNIFICANT problems or challenges your Icon experienced with regard to no one or very few people recognizing, pointing out or developing abilities, talents or skills in him or her.

1._____
_____
_____
_____
_____
_____

2._____
_____
_____
_____
_____
_____

3._____
_____
_____
_____
_____
_____

4._____
_____
_____
_____
_____
_____

SUCCESS WORKSHEET #1

As you read the autobiography, SELECT at least two (2) examples of persons, things or experiences that helped to identify and develop abilities, talents or skills of your Icon. Explain how each example eventually contributed to your Icon's success.

PERSON, THING or EXPERIENCE

1._____

_____

_____

_____

_____

_____

_____

2._____

_____

_____

_____

_____

_____

_____

3._____

_____

_____

_____

_____

_____

_____

2

AMBITION IGNITION

AMBITION IGNITION: The requirement for someone or something to initiate, generate and sustain motivation, inspiration, dreams or goals in a person's life. Behind determination is an attitude of "I will" that was preceded by the attitude of "I want".

Example of an Icon with Many Problems: Ann Richards was a sickly child who grew up in a town in which it was believed that females were inferior and activities and dreams should be limited.

Example of Solution: Ann Richards' father raised her to believe she could do anything a boy could do and her school had Debate Clubs. Confidence and debating skills eventually helped her become the first female Governor of Texas.

PROBLEM INVENTORY #2

List and explain two (2) MAJOR problems or challenges your Icon experienced because of an environment in which there was an absence of or limited exposure to positive activities, experiences or role models who made him or her want to set goals or dream of what was possible for their future.

1._____
_____
_____
_____
_____
_____

2._____
_____
_____
_____
_____
_____

3._____
_____
_____
_____
_____
_____

4._____
_____
_____
_____
_____
_____

SUCCESS WORKSHEET #2

As you read the autobiography, SELECT at least two (2) examples of persons, things or experiences that led your Icon to set goals or have dreams of what was possible. Explain how each example eventually contributed to your Icon's success.

PERSON, THING or EXPERIENCE

1._____

_____

_____

_____

_____

_____

_____

2._____

_____

_____

_____

_____

_____

_____

3._____

_____

_____

_____

_____

_____

_____

_____

3

CARDIAC RESERVE

CARDIAC RESERVE: The requirement for someone or something to cause a person to feel valued, loved or important. The emotional heart must be maintained with enough reserves of warmth and worth to prevent or heal emotional damage.

Example of an Icon with Many Problems: Jamie Foxx was abandoned by his parents who were not willing to be responsible for raising and caring for him.

Example of Solution: Jamie Foxx's Grandmother adopted him and engaged him in activities such as piano lessons which contributed to his becoming a musician and Oscar-winning actor.

PROBLEM INVENTORY #3

List and briefly explain at least two (2) of the MAJOR or SIGNIFICANT problems or challenges in an environment which was missing the types of treatment or expressions to make your Icon feel loved, valued or special.

1._____
_____
_____
_____
_____
_____

2._____
_____
_____
_____
_____
_____

3._____
_____
_____
_____
_____
_____

4._____
_____
_____
_____
_____
_____

SUCCESS WORKSHEET #3

As you read the autobiography, SELECT three examples of persons, things or experiences that made your Icon feel important, special and/or loved. Explain how each example eventually contributed to your Icon's success.

PERSON, THING or EXPERIENCE

1._____
_____
_____
_____
_____
_____
_____
_____

2._____
_____
_____
_____
_____
_____
_____
_____

3._____
_____
_____
_____
_____
_____
_____
_____
_____

4

APEX NERVE

APEX NERVE: The requirement for someone or something to demand and instruct for performance at a level of excellence. It requires someone or something to "push" a person. Excellence training is the development of proficiency or virtuosity rather than mere functionality. It is essential for maximizing potential.

Example of an Icon with Many Problems: Helen Keller was pitied and never challenged by her family because she could not hear nor see nor speak.

Example of Solution: Helen Keller's teacher, Anne Sullivan, did not pity Helen but rather challenged her to learn. That strategy and turning point resulted in Helen's life of brilliance and fame.

PROBLEM INVENTORY #4

List and briefly explain at least two (2) of the MAJOR or SIGNIFICANT problems or challenges your Icon experienced in an environment that lacked a demand for best performance or excellence. Merely "good enough" or mediocrity was acceptable.

1._____
_____
_____
_____
_____
_____

2._____
_____
_____
_____
_____
_____

3._____
_____
_____
_____
_____
_____

4._____
_____
_____
_____
_____
_____

SUCCESS WORKSHEET #4

As you read the autobiography, SELECT at least two (2) examples of persons, things or experiences that were strong enough to instill standards of excellence or "pushed" the ACHIEVER for peak performance. Explain how each example eventually contributed to your Icon's success.

PERSON, THING or EXPERIENCE

1._____

_____

_____

_____

_____

_____

_____

2._____

_____

_____

_____

_____

_____

_____

_____

3._____

_____

_____

_____

_____

_____

_____

_____

_____

5

INSIGHT TRAMS

INSIGHT TRAMS: The requirement for someone or something to move a person forward or closer to their dreams and goals by teaching them how to grow deeper in academic, emotional, financial or spiritual understanding. Progress toward success is proportionate to the amount of insight gained.

Example of an Icon with Many Problems: During Nelson Mandela's childhood, his family had financial problems which initially limited the quality of his education and training.

Example of Solution: Mandela's transfer to his Uncle's home exposed him to "royalty training" from which he gained skill sets and a strong sense of self which sustained him through 27 years of political imprisonment and later propelled him to global success.

PROBLEM INVENTORY #5

List and briefly explain at least two (2) of the MAJOR or SIGNIFICANT problems or challenges in an environment where learning was limited to memorizing or surface knowledge or where there was a lack awareness or exploration of how things work.

1._____
_____
_____
_____
_____
_____

2._____
_____
_____
_____
_____

3._____
_____
_____
_____
_____

4._____
_____
_____
_____
_____
_____

SUCCESS WORKSHEET #5

As you read the autobiography, SELECT at least two (2) examples of persons, things or experiences that moved your Icon forward by teaching him or her how to think at higher levels and/or explore deeper into academic, social, financial or spiritual understanding. Explain how each example eventually contributed to your Icon's success.

PERSON, THING or EXPERIENCE

1._____

_____

_____

_____

_____

_____

_____

_____

2._____

_____

_____

_____

_____

_____

_____

_____

3._____

_____

_____

_____

_____

_____

_____

_____

_____

6

OPPORTUNITY RAMS

OPPORTUNITY RAMS: The requirement for someone or something to provide awareness of or resources for opportunities to assist with destroying obstacles to a person's progress. The existence of opportunity is useless for those who have neither awareness of nor access to those opportunities.

Example of an Icon with Many Problems: Even with all of his genius, Albert Einstein was depressed by a denial of his major career goal which was a teaching position at Zurich.

Example of Solution: Einstein's colleague, Marcel Grossman, remembered his genius friend and helped him get a job at a patent office. During that active period, Einstein formulated the "Theory of Relativity" for which he won the Nobel Prize in Science.

PROBLEM INVENTORY #6

List and briefly explain at least two (2) of the MAJOR or SIGNIFICANT problems or challenges which your Icon had regarding lack of awareness of opportunities or lack of resources for gaining opportunities to get to a better future.

1._____
_____
_____
_____
_____
_____

2._____
_____
_____
_____
_____

3._____
_____
_____
_____
_____

4._____
_____
_____
_____
_____

SUCCESS WORKSHEET #6

As you read the autobiography, SELECT at least two (2) examples of persons, things or experiences that provided opportunities for or destroyed obstacles to the progress of your Icon. Explain how each example eventually contributed to your Icon's success.

PERSON, THING or EXPERIENCE

1._____

_____

_____

_____

_____

_____

_____

2._____

_____

_____

_____

_____

_____

_____

3._____

_____

_____

_____

_____

_____

_____

_____

SCRIPT #1 FOR YOUR ICON'S NEW LIFE

(What Might Have Happened)

<u>Directions</u>: Re-make your Icon's life by doing the following: Go back and choose one of the success factors which you identified on the *Success Worksheets* and IMAGINE what could have happened if that factor had not been part of the Icon's life. Re-write the outcomes and the ending of your Icon's life story by describing what could have happened without that factor. Follow the steps below.

The person, thing or experience that I will REMOVE is based on a Worksheet in the following category:

      _____ <u>Ability Nutrition</u>   _____ <u>Ambition Ignition</u>

      _____ <u>Cardiac Reserve</u>   _____ <u>Apex Nerve</u>

      _____ <u>Insight Trams</u>   _____ <u>Opportunity Rams</u>

_____

_____

_____

_____

_____

_____

_____

_____

_____

_____

_____

If my Icon HAD NOT HAD that factor in his or her life, then this person's life would have been different. The following events or changes might have taken place:

_____
_____
_____
_____
_____
_____
_____
_____
_____
_____
_____
_____
_____
_____

Finally, **CREATE** something original, such as a skit, rap, poem, hashtag, power-point, music, or visual art about your Icon. **SHARE** your creation in a small group or in a Talent Show.

_____
_____
_____
_____
_____
_____
_____
_____
_____
_____

SCRIPT #2 FOR YOUR ICON'S NEW LIFE

(What Might Have Happened)

Directions: Re-make your Icon's life by doing the following: Go back and choose one of the success factors which you identified on the *Success Worksheets* and IMAGINE what could have happened if that factor had not been part of the Icon's life. Re-write the outcomes and the ending of your Icon's life story by describing what could have happened without that factor. Follow the steps below.

The person, thing or experience that I will REMOVE is based on a Worksheet in the following category:

_____ Ability Nutrition	_____ Ambition Ignition
_____ Cardiac Reserve	_____ Apex Nerve
_____ Insight Trams	_____ Opportunity Rams

_____

_____

_____

_____

_____

_____

_____

_____

_____

If my Icon HAD NOT HAD that factor in his or her life, then this person's life would have been different. The following events or changes might have taken place:

_____

_____

_____

_____

_____

_____

_____

_____

_____

_____

_____

_____

_____

_____

_____

_____

_____

_____

_____

_____

Finally, **CREATE** something original, such as a skit, rap, poem, hashtag, power-point, music, or visual art about your Icon. **SHARE** your creation in a small group or in a Talent Show.

_____

_____

_____

_____

_____

_____

_____

_____

_____

SCRIPT #3 FOR YOUR ICON'S NEW LIFE

(What Might Have Happened)

<u>Directions</u>: Re-make your Icon's life by doing the following: Go back and choose one of the success factors which you identified on the *Success Worksheets* and IMAGINE what could have happened if that factor had not been part of the Icon's life. Re-write the outcomes and the ending of your Icon's life story by describing what could have happened without that factor. Follow the steps below.

The person, thing or experience that I will REMOVE is based on a Worksheet in the following category:

____	Ability Nutrition	____	Ambition Ignition
____	Cardiac Reserve	____	Apex Nerve
____	Insight Trams	____	Opportunity Rams

_____

_____

_____

_____

_____

_____

_____

_____

_____

_____

If my Icon HAD NOT HAD that factor in his or her life, then this person's life would have been different. The following events or changes might have taken place:

_____

_____

_____

_____

_____

_____

_____

_____

_____

_____

_____

_____

_____

_____

_____

_____

_____

_____

_____

_____

Finally, **CREATE** something original, such as a skit, rap, poem, hashtag, power-point, music, or visual art about your Icon. **SHARE** your creation in a small group or in a Talent Show.

_____

_____

_____

_____

_____

_____

_____

_____

_____

EXIT TICKET #1

REFLECTIONS FROM THE STUDY OF YOUR ICON

Lessons You Learned

1._____

_____

_____

_____

2._____

_____

_____

_____

3._____

_____

_____

_____

4._____

_____

_____

_____

5._____

_____

_____

_____

Reflections (Continued)

6._____

_____

_____

_____

7._____

_____

_____

_____

8._____

_____

_____

_____

9._____

_____

_____

_____

10._____

_____

_____

_____

PART II

ALL ABOUT YOUR SUCCESS

Look Within and Then Look Forward

On this day, as the world watches your sojourn here,
I ask with simple courtesy, "Have you looked within yourself?"
If you had, then you would know who you are
and that you stand on the shoulders of all your ancestors
who have prepared the path for your journey.
Look within, and then look forward.
I know that today's pressures are awesome,
but have you tested your own strength of character?
It may be that you have no knowledge
of the roots from which you came
nor the shoulders on which you stand today.
Study the history of your people.
Those individuals faced forces far greater than today's pressures,
and yet they were not deterred
from making positive contributions to the world.
My son and my daughter,
you did not get to this moment in life alone.
As the one who carries the DNA of the forefathers,
you cannot deny your birthright.
Your task, on this day of enlightenment, is to study your history
And heritage so you will know better, to do better.
Look within and then look forward, to greatness.

1

ABILITY NUTRITION

Success Worksheet #1

In the space below, identify persons, things or experiences that helped YOU to develop your abilities or skills. These can be examples from your past or present. If you have not found any of the "building materials" in this category yet, then describe who or what you think might help with this in the future.

PERSON, THING or EXPERIENCE

1. What skills, abilities and talents did you think you were missing until someone or something made you recognize abilities in you?

_____

_____

_____

_____

_____

_____

_____

_____

_____

_____

2. During the past, who or what has helped you develop or expand those skills, abilities or talents?

_____

_____

_____

_____

_____

_____

_____

_____

_____

_____

_____

_____

_____

_____

3. In the future, what types of people, things or experiences do you think you need to search for in order to develop or improve your abilities, skills, gifts or talents?

_____

_____

_____

_____

_____

_____

_____

_____

_____

_____

_____

_____

_____

_____

_____

2

AMBITION IGNITION

SUCCESS WORKSHEET #2

In the space below, identify persons, things or experiences that led YOU
to set and strive for goals or motivated you to dream bigger. They can be
examples from your past or present. If you have not found any of this type
of building block yet, describe who or what you think it might be in the
future.

PERSON, THING or EXPERIENCE

1. What goals or dreams were you missing until someone or something
made you realize what is possible for you, regarding school, your career or
your life in general?

_____

_____

_____

_____

_____

_____

_____

2. Who or what has helped you set goals and have dreams? Who or what
has motivated you to keep going in spite of any obstacles? Who are your
role models?

_____

_____

_____

_____

_____

_____

_____

_____

_____

_____

_____

_____

_____

3. In the future, what people, things or experiences do you think you need to search for in order to help you continue to set goals and strive to achieve them?

_____

_____

_____

_____

_____

_____

_____

_____

_____

_____

_____

_____

_____

_____

3

CARDIAC RESERVE

SUCCESS WORKSHEET #3

In the space below, identify persons, things or experiences that made or make YOU feel important, special and/or loved. They can be examples from your past or present. If you have not found any of this type of building block yet, describe who or what you think it might be in the future.

PERSON, THING or EXPERIENCE

1. Did you ever feel as though you were not special or worthy or loved until someone made you realize that you were special?

_____

_____

_____

_____

_____

_____

_____

_____

2. In the past, what persons, events, things or experiences made you feel special or loved?

_____

_____

_____

_____

_____

_____

_____

_____

_____

_____

_____

_____

_____

3. In the future, who or what do you need to seek in order to make you feel or keep you feeling special, worthy, or loved? _____

_____

_____

_____

_____

_____

_____

_____

_____

_____

_____

_____

_____

_____

_____

4

APEX NERVE

SUCCESS WORKSHEET #4

In the space below, identify persons or experiences that were strong enough to instill standards of excellence or "pushed" YOU to achieve at your top level. They can be examples from your past or present. If you have not found any of this type of building block yet, describe who or what you think it might be in the future.

PERSON, THING or EXPERIENCE

1. Did you ever think you were doing well enough at home, at school, at work, until someone made you aware that you could do much better or perform better?

_____

_____

_____

_____

_____

_____

_____

_____

_____

_____

_____

_____

_____

_____

2. During the past, who "pushed" you to do better or reach for a level of excellence in school, at work or in life?

_____
_____
_____
_____
_____
_____
_____
_____
_____
_____
_____
_____

3. In the future, who or what do you think you need to seek that will help you stay motivated to perform at your highest level?

_____
_____
_____
_____
_____
_____
_____
_____
_____
_____
_____
_____
_____
_____

5

INSIGHT TRAMS

SUCCESS WORKSHEET #5

In the space below, identify persons or experiences that moved YOU forward or closer to your goals by teaching you <u>how to</u> grow in academic, emotional, financial or spiritual understanding. They can be examples from your past or present. If you have not found any of this type of building block yet, describe who or what you think it might be in the future.

PERSON, THING or EXPERIENCE

1. Who or what is currently helping you learn at a deep level so that you can use your knowledge? Who or what is helping you understand things and yourself in new ways?

_____

_____

_____

_____

_____

_____

_____

_____

_____

_____

_____

_____

_____

_____

_____
_____
_____

2. During the past, who or what has provided new insight for you in school and in life?

_____
_____
_____
_____
_____
_____
_____
_____
_____
_____
_____
_____
_____

3. Who or what do you think you need to seek in order to increase your knowledge and expand your ability to do more in your life?

_____
_____
_____
_____
_____
_____
_____
_____
_____
_____

6

OPPORTUNITY RAMS

SUCCESS WORKSHEET #6

In the space below, identify persons or experiences that provided opportunities for YOU or destroyed obstacles to YOUR progress. They can be examples from your past or present. If you have not found any of this type of building block yet, describe who or what you think it might be in the future.

PERSON, THING or EXPERIENCE

1. Who are the people providing opportunities for you at the present time? Has someone or something prevented an obstacle from getting in the way of your current progress?

_____

_____

_____

_____

_____

_____

_____

_____

_____

_____

_____

_____

_____

_____

_____

_____

_____

_____

2. What past opportunities have you had and who or what created those opportunities? Is there anything in your past that would have hindered your progress? Who or what prevented that from happening or helped you overcome the obstacles?

_____

_____

_____

_____

_____

_____

_____

_____

_____

_____

_____

_____

3. What persons, things or experiences can you seek which will be helpful to you in gaining access to future opportunities? Who or what can you seek to help you destroy future obstacles that might block your success.

_____

_____

_____

_____

_____

_____

_____

_____

EXIT TICKET #2

REFLECTIONS FROM STUDYING YOURSELF

Lessons You Learned

1._____
_____
_____
_____

2._____
_____
_____
_____

3._____
_____
_____
_____

4._____
_____
_____
_____

5._____
_____
_____
_____

Reflections (Continued)

6._____

_____

_____

_____

7._____

_____

_____

_____

8._____

_____

_____

_____

9._____

_____

_____

_____

10._____

_____

_____

_____

PART III

USING YOUR LESSONS TO HELP OTHERS

**Take Yourself
to the Appraisers**

You are a diamond!
You are brilliant, beautiful,
strong, prismatic,
and precious.

But when you are made
to feel deficient,
depreciated or discolored,
Forget what observers say.
Forget what buyers pay.
Take yourself
to the appraisers
to determine
your *immeasurable* value.
The appraisers are
loved ones who
cherish you,
friends who choose you,
leaders who inspire you.
Better, yet, get
the ultimate
vision of yourself:
Take yourself to the
JEWEL CREATOR!
© Nanthalia W. McJamerson

An Icon Gives Back. Icons reach out to help others.

Adaryll Moore

1

ABILITY NUTRITION

How can I identify or help develop an ability,
talent or skill in someone's life?

1._____

_____

_____

_____

_____

_____

2._____

_____

_____

_____

_____

_____

3._____

_____

_____

_____

_____

_____

_____

2

AMBITION IGNITION

How can I get someone excited about setting or
reaching their goals or dreaming big?

1._____

_____

_____

_____

_____

_____

_____

2._____

_____

_____

_____

_____

_____

_____

3._____

_____

_____

_____

_____

_____

_____

3

CARDIAC RESERVE

How can I make someone feel important, loved, valued or special?

1._____

_____

_____

_____

_____

_____

_____

_____

2._____

_____

_____

_____

_____

_____

_____

_____

3._____

_____

_____

_____

_____

_____

_____

_____

4

APEX NERVE

How can I teach or "push" someone to perform at a
level of excellence or at their highest level?

1._____

_____

_____

_____

_____

_____

_____

2._____

_____

_____

_____

_____

_____

_____

3._____

_____

_____

_____

_____

_____

_____

5

INSIGHT TRAMS

How can I help someone gain deeper understanding in academic, social, spiritual or financial areas of life?

1._____

_____

_____

_____

_____

_____

_____

_____

2._____

_____

_____

_____

_____

_____

_____

_____

3._____

_____

_____

_____

_____

_____

_____

_____

6

OPPORTUNITY RAMS

How can I provide an opportunity for someone to move forward,
or how can I assist in destroying obstacles to someone's progress?

1._____
_____
_____
_____
_____
_____
_____
_____

2._____
_____
_____
_____
_____
_____
_____
_____

3._____
_____
_____
_____
_____
_____

SOME AUTOBIOGRAPHIES
TO CONSIDER

Dr. Maya Angelou *I Know Why the Caged Bird Sings*

Beyoncé Knowles *Beyonce: Running the World: A Biography*
(Anna Pointer)

Christy Brown *My Left Foot or The Christy Brown Story*

Dr. Ben Carson *Gifted Hands: The Ben Carson Story*
(Ben Carson & Cecil Murphey)

Cesar Chavez *Cesar Chavez: Autobiography of La Causa*
(Jacques E. Levy & Barbara Moulton)

Hillary Clinton *Living History*

Bessie Coleman *Queen Bess: Daredevil Aviator*
(Doris & Mae Jemison)

Dr. Marie Curie *Madame Currie: A Biography*
(Eve Currie)

Fyodor Dostoevsky *Dostoevsky: A Writer in His Time*
(Joseph Frank)

Albert Einstein *Albert Einstein: A Biography*
(Albrecht Folsing)

Anne Frank *Anne Frank: The Diary of a Young Girl*

Patrice Gaines *Laughing in the Dark*

William "Bill" Gates *Hard Drive: Bill Gates and the Making of The Microsoft Empire*
(James Wallace & Jim Erickson)

Chris Gardner *The Pursuit of Happyness*
(Chris Gardner & Quincy Troupe)

Linda Hogan *Woman Who Watches Over The World: A Native Memoir*

Dr. Mae Jemison	*Find Where the Wind Goes: Moments from My Life*
John H. Johnson	*Succeeding Against the Odds*
Helen Keller	*The Story of My Life*
Edward Kennedy	*True Compass: A Memoir*
Dr. Martin Luther King, Jr.	*The Autobiography of Martin Luther King, Jr.* (M. King, Jr. & Clayborne Carson)
LL Cool J (James T. Smith)	*I Make My Own Rules* (James Todd Smith & Karen Hunter)
Nelson Mandela	*A Long Walk to Freedom: The Autobiography of Nelson Mandela*
Justice Thurgood Marshall	*Dream Maker, Dream Breaker* (Carl Rowan)
Judge Gregory Mathis	*Inner City Miracle*
Janet Mock	*Redefining Realness: My Path to Womanhood, Identity, Love and So Much More*
President Barack H. Obama	*Dreams from My Father: A Story of Race and Inheritance*
Michelle Obama	*Becoming Michelle Obama*
Governor Ann Richards	*Thorny Rose of Texas* (Shropshire, M. & Schaefer, F.)
Dr. Eddie Robinson, Sr. (Eddie Robinson & Richard Lapchick)	*Never Before, Never Again*
Wilma Rudolph	*Wilma Rudolph: A Biography* (Maureen Margaret Smith)
Tupac Amaru Shakur	*Holler If You Hear Me* (Michael Eric Dyson)
Sonia Sotomayor	*My Beloved World*
Oprah Winfrey	*Oprah!* (Robert Waldron)

BIBLIOGRAPHY

Akbar., N. (1995). *Natural psychology and human transformation.* Tallahassee, FL: Mind Productions and Associates.

Bandura, A. (1997). *Self-efficacy: The exercise of control.* New York: W. H. Freeman.

Berlak, A., & Berlak, H. (1981). *The dilemmas of schooling.* London: Methuen.

Beyer, L. E. (1979). *Schools, aesthetic forms, and social reproduction.* Madison: University of Wisconsin.

Bronfenbrenner, U. (2000). "Developmental science in the 21st century: Emerging questions, theoretical models, research designs and empirical findings." *Social Development,* 9, 115-125.

Comer, J., Ben-Avie, M., Haynes, N., and Joyner, E. (1999). *Child by Child: The Comer process for change in education.* New York: Teachers College Press.

Covington, M. V. (1992). *Making the grade: A self-worth perspective on motivation and school reform. New York: Holt, Rinehart and Winston.*

Darling-Hammond, L. (1995). "Inequality and access to knowledge." In J. A. Banks, C. M. Banks, Eds. *Handbook of research on multicultural education.* New York: Macmillan Publishing USA.

Freire, P. (1973). *Pedagogy of the oppressed.* New York: Seabury.

Glaser, B., and Strauss, A. (1976). *The discovery of grounded theory: strategies for qualitative research.* Chicago: Aldine.

Hale, J. (1994). *Unbank the fire: Visions for the education of African-American children.* Baltimore: The Johns Hopkins University Press.

Hammond, Z. (2015). *Culturally Responsive Teaching and the Brain: Promoting Authentic Engagement and Rigor Among Culturally and Linguistically Diverse Students.* Thousand Oaks, CA: Corwin.

Jaggers, L., McJamerson, N. and Duhon, G. (2000). *Developing literacy skills across the curriculum.* New York: Mellen Press.

Kunjufu, J. (1986). *Motivating and preparing Black youth for success.* Chicago, IL: African American Images.

Ladson-Billings, G. (1997). *Dream keepers: Successful teachers of African American children*. San Francisco: Jossey-Bass Publishing Co.

Maslow, A. H. (1998). *Toward a psychology of being. New York: John Wiley & Sons*.

McJamerson, J. (2015). *On the Shoulders of Our Ancestors: African American History through Historical Poetic Verse*. Ruston, LA: McJamerson Achiever Builders.

McJamerson, N. (2016). Reconstructing Lives: *Taking the Mystery out of Success*. Staten Island, NY: Page Publishing.

Santrock, J. W. (2016). *Life-Span development*. Columbus, OH: McGraw-Hill Publishing Company.

Shor, I. (1980). *Critical thinking and everyday life*. Boston: South End Press.

Swadener, B., and Lubeck, S. (Eds.). (1995). *Children and families "at promise": Deconstructing the discourse of at-risk*. Albany: State University of New York Press.

Werner, E. (1996). "How kids become resilient: Observations and cautions." *Resiliency in Action, 1(1)*, 18-28.

ABOUT THE AUTHOR

Dr. Nanthalia McJamerson is a retired Professor of Education from Grambling State University. She also served as a Visiting Professor at South Carolina State University and a researcher at CEMREL at St. Louis. Her books include a success guide titled *Reconstructing Lives: Taking the Mystery out of Success* and a poetry collection, *Contrary to Rumor, I'm Wonderfully Made.* Her philanthropy involves sponsoring local school activities and scholarships at GSU in honor of her husband, *the late* Dr. Jimmy McJamerson. Motivational Speaker, Mentor and Consultant are among her titles. One of Dr. McJamerson's greatest joys was working as Co-Director for the GSU LA GEAR UP Summer Learning Camps for youth, 2005-2012. As Co-Founder of the McJamerson Consulting Company (www.buildanachiever.com), she was given the title "General Contractor for Building Achievers."

Special Acknowledgments to
Tim & Lisa Martin, Entrepreneurs
Dr. Kathy Newman, Professor of Education
Dr. Gwendolyn Duhon, Professor of Education
Dr. Felicie Barnes, Co-Developer/Facilitator
Dr. A. Kadir Nur-Hussen, Project Facilitator
Dr. Pamela M. Payne, Associate Professor, Principal
Lee Johnson, Sr., Educator/Retired
Adaryll Moore, Author/Consultant
James Penny, J. E. Penny Communications Group

CONTACT INFORMATION
McJamerson Achiever Builders
P. O. Box 2881
Ruston, LA 71273

Email: nmcjamerson1@gmail.com
Website: www.buildanachiever.com

Printed in the United States
By Bookmasters